D1259438

CONTEMPORARY LIVES

LIL WAYNE

GRAMMY-WINNING HIP-HOP ARTIST

ABDO
Publishing Company

CONTEMPORARY LIVES

LIL WAYNE

GRAMMY-WINNING HIP-HOP ARTIST

by Erika Wittekind

CREDITS

Published by ABDO Publishing Company, PO Box 398166, Minneapolis, MN 55439. Copyright © 2014 by Abdo Consulting Group, Inc. International copyrights reserved in all countries. No part of this book may be reproduced in any form without written permission from the publisher. The Essential Library™ is a trademark and logo of ABDO Publishing Company.

Printed in the United States of America,
North Mankato, Minnesota
082013
012014

 THIS BOOK CONTAINS AT LEAST 10% RECYCLED MATERIALS.

Editor: Melissa York
Series Designer: Emily Love

Photo credits: Jordan Strauss/Invision/AP Images, cover, 3, 74; Robert E. Klein/AP Images, 6; Mark J. Terrill/AP Images, 10; Kevin Winter/Getty Images, 16; Seth Poppel/Yearbook Library, 18, 27, 96 (left); Infrogmation, 23; Tony Gutierrez/AP Images, 28, 96 (right); Ron Galella, Ltd./Getty Images, 32; Kevin Knight/Corbis, 35; Charles Sykes/Invision/AP Images, 36; Paul Hebert/Icon SMI, 42; Jeff Daly/Invision/AP Images, 44, 100; Jim Cooper/AP Images, 50; Eric Gay/AP Images, 52, 98 (top); Valerie Macon/Getty Images, 55, 97; Dana Edelson/NBC/NBCU Photo Bank/Getty Images, 60; John Shearer/WireImage/Getty Images, 62, 99 (top); Frank Micelotta/Invsion/AP Images, 65; Rahav Segev/Photopass/Alamy, 69; Louis Lanzano/AP Images, 73, 98 (bottom); Prince Williams/FilmMagic/Getty Images, 80; Cash Money/Universal Records/AP Images, 82, 99 (bottom); Cash Money/Young Money/Universal Republic/AP Images, 84; Katy Winn/Invision/AP Images, 86; Gerald Herbert/AP Images, 92; Chris Pizzello/AP Images, 95

Library of Congress Control Number: 2013946066

Cataloging-in-Publication Data

Wittekind, Erika.
 Lil Wayne: Grammy-winning hip-hop artist / Erika Wittekind.
   p. cm. -- (Contemporary lives)
Includes bibliographical references and index.
ISBN 978-1-62403-229-5
1. Lil Wayne--Juvenile literature. 2. Rap musicians--United States--Biography--Juvenile literature. 1. Title.
782.421649092--dc23
[B]
                                                          2013946066

CONTENTS

Lil Wayne is known for his artistic and clever raps.

CHAPTER 1
"Best Rapper Alive"

||||||||||||||||||||||||||||||||||

I n 2007, Lil Wayne was on the edge of superstardom. Hip-hop journalists at the cable television network MTV had named him "the hottest m.c. in the game."[1] When he wasn't touring, he was cranking out music in the recording studio, sometimes recording up to three or four songs in one night. Lil Wayne was so prolific, *Vibe* magazine was able to compile a list of his 77 best songs of 2007. Meanwhile, big-time rappers including Kanye West—who Lil Wayne was surprised even knew who he was—were personally calling up Lil Wayne, wanting to record with him. The growing consensus among those in the know was that Lil Wayne, at the age of 24, wasn't so little anymore. "In four years, Lil Wayne has evolved from a fairly predictable Southern gangsta rapper into an artist who may actually deserve the bragging rights to 'best rapper alive,' his current motto," declared an article in *New Yorker* magazine.[2]

Others, however, were starting to wonder if the rapper could live up to so much hype. In 2004, his breakout fourth solo album, *Tha Carter,* reached Number 5 on the *Billboard* Hot 100. He quickly

WORLD'S GREATEST RAPPER |||||||||||||||||||||||||||||||||||||||||||||||||||||

In December 2006, Lil Wayne made waves in the hip-hop world when he declared he had surpassed Jay Z as the world's greatest rapper. "It's not your house anymore and I'm better than you," he said to Jay Z through an interview with the hip-hop magazine *Complex.*[3] Afterward, the two exchanged criticisms of each other while rapping on the tracks of other artists. Jay Z made fun of Lil Wayne for smoking marijuana, while Lil Wayne took shots at his then 37-year-old rival for his age.

followed that success with *Tha Carter II* in 2005. Beloved by critics and fans alike, the album sold more than 1.8 million copies.[4] Although his name and music seemed to be almost everywhere—from free releases making their rounds on the Internet to guest appearances in other artists' music—the next two years passed without Lil Wayne releasing a single or an album in his own name. Music critic Steve Jones wrote about the buildup in *USA Today*:

> *[Lil Wayne's] frequently delayed sixth album faces a near-impossible task of living up to its hype. It's arguably the most anticipated rap album of 2007 and 2008. But after several mixtapes and featured appearances flooded the market and countless leaked tracks were voraciously consumed on the Internet, you had to wonder if he had enough left to deliver the goods.[5]*

Lil Wayne pointed to the amount of attention he still received two years after *Tha Carter II* had come out. "I don't know what they're gonna do when the [next] album drops. Y'all are probably gonna say, 'Everybody else stop rapping,'" he joked to an MTV journalist.[6]

Lil Wayne, *bottom right*, has collaborated with, *from left*, Kanye West, T.I., and Jay Z.

PART OF THE CONVERSATION

While he took his time perfecting what would be the third installment of the Tha Carter series, Lil Wayne was very deliberate about keeping his name in the hip-hop conversation. In addition to appearing on more than 100 tracks—recording at least one track with nearly every major rapper—he released his own music on mixtapes. While rappers had long used mixtapes as a way to publicize their names and music or to keep in touch with fans, Lil Wayne delivered an unusually large amount of popular music through this form. He released four double album–length mixtapes and numerous singles in two years. Critics said the releases included some of Lil Wayne's best music yet and praised his innovative use of mixtapes as a marketing strategy. "By posting his songs for free on the Internet and, in the process, acquiring new fans, he is proving that the established methods of distribution, like the established rappers, no longer rule," noted the *New Yorker* in 2007.[7] The artist had nothing but confidence his somewhat unusual marketing strategies would pay off.

Why release so much music for free? Some of it would have presented legal difficulties to release officially because, similar to a lot of underground rap music, it used samples of other musicians' music and beats without their permission. It also allowed Lil Wayne more freedom to put out the music he wanted in an unfiltered way and to be picky about which of the many tracks he produced would end up on the album. Some of his music, however, was taken without his consent. Tracks that had been earmarked for *Tha Carter III* started appearing on the Internet, but Lil Wayne took the news in stride. "Between the bootleggers, the downloading, and someone leaking my music to both, I had to come to an understanding of the world changing," he said. "If I can't beat them,

MIXTAPES

Rappers have been putting out mixtapes since the 1970s, even before hip-hop music was recorded and distributed through labels. The first mixtapes were cassettes compiled by DJs. Now they are distributed as CDs and downloadable files. The mixes can include unreleased or exclusive music by well-known or new artists; freestyle performances using borrowed beats from other music; or songs mixed, blended, or altered by a DJ. Without a studio or label involved, the results are considered more authentic and unfiltered. "Mixtapes are incredible because they're straight from a brother's heart," rapper LL Cool J told MTV. "Music that they really feel, not music that just researches well. That's special, and that's my favorite way to listen to music: mixtapes."[8]

The unofficial albums circulate on street corners, through bootleggers, and on the Internet. Hip-hop hopefuls try to appear on mixtapes to get their names in the public, while established artists often still release mixes as a way to communicate more directly with established fans and reach new audiences. "I saturate the street market because mixtapes are the entry level of hip-hop," rapper 50 Cent said.[9]

I'll join them."[10] In a June 2007 YouTube video, he announced he would release the free mixtape *The Leak*, which contained the leaked music. The move earned him even more goodwill from fans, although replacing the leaked music delayed the release of the sixth solo record even more.

Meanwhile, some at Lil Wayne's record label were starting to worry their promising recording artist was giving away too much. Why would anyone pay for the music when they could already access so much of it for free? Sylvia Rhone, an executive at the major record label Universal Motown, which was partnering with Cash Money Records to put out Lil Wayne's sixth album, said the release of so many mixtapes was a concern, but the label still expected the album to do well. "It really goes counter to what we would like our artists to do, but I think in this case we have this 'Wayne mania,' even though he hasn't released a record in over two years," Rhone said.[11]

In the months leading up to *Tha Carter III*'s debut, Lil Wayne's tracks were the most pirated on peer-to-peer file sharing networks, according to BigChampagne, a company that monitors such traffic. Each downloader of Lil Wayne's music was

Ron Williams, cofounder of Lil Wayne's first record label, Cash Money Records, had confidence his protégé's sixth album would be a massive hit. He even predicted it would sell more than 1 million copies in the first week. "I've been saying a million all along, and I've been telling people, and they've been looking at me crazy," Williams said. "He worked hard. He just came with something different. He let his skills show on a lot of mixtapes. He's featured on a lot of people's records. It just made people anticipate his record more than ever."[13]

taking an average of ten of his tracks, compared to an average of two tracks taken by the downloaders of other artists. Eric Garland, chief executive of BigChampagne, saw that as a positive sign for Lil Wayne because it spoke to the seriousness of his following. "While people who like an individual song are not going to open their wallets for you, people who like 10 songs will. I think the mixtape phenomenon is great for feeding the machine, which is what the music industry is about in the 21st century," Garland said.[12]

Lil Wayne's lack of possessiveness toward his music paid off, building his fans into a frenzy before his album's release. After he settled on 16 tracks for *Tha Carter III*—including the breakout pop hit "Lollipop"—the album was finally released on June 10, 2008, and sold 423,000 copies in its first day.[14] It surpassed 1 million copies in its first week.[15] With CD sales declining for all genres of music, the milestone was especially notable. No other album had passed the 1 million mark in its first week of release since 2005, when 50 Cent's *The Massacre* sold 1.1 million.[18] Eventually selling more than 2.8 million copies, *Tha Carter III*

PRAISE FOR *THA CARTER III*

At the same time it was flying off the shelves, Lil Wayne's long-awaited *Tha Carter III* was also critically acclaimed. "The New Orleans rapper doesn't just spew clever lines on topics ranging from his place in the hip-hop hierarchy to post-Katrina governmental neglect and obstacles to rising from poverty," music reviewer Steve Jones wrote in *USA Today*. "He uses innovative song structures and concepts while taking advantage of the colorful sonic palette provided by top-flight producers."[16]

Author and music writer Ben Westhoff had good things to say as well. "The album [*Tha Carter III*] deserved its success; it is at turns mischievous, bizarre, rambling, and tragic, everything that is crass and wonderful about rap music. Featuring beats tailor-made for his slow improv-heavy verses, it contains both radio-friendly melodies and weird, off-kilter ones that stop and start abruptly."[17]

Lil Wayne accepted the Best Hip Hop Video Award for "Lollipop" at the 2008 MTV Video Music Awards with artist T-Pain.

became the best-selling album of 2008.[19] Lil Wayne had long felt he was sitting at the top of the rap world. Now he had the numbers to back it up.

|||||||||||

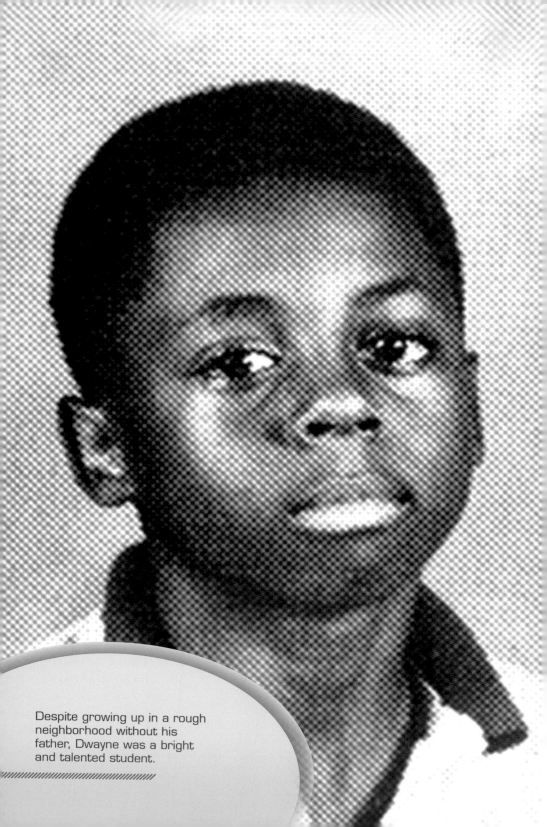

Despite growing up in a rough neighborhood without his father, Dwayne was a bright and talented student.

CHAPTER 2
Early Life

||||||||||||||||||||||||||||||||||||||||||||||||||||||||||||||||||

L il Wayne was born Dwayne Michael Carter Jr. on September 27, 1982, in New Orleans, Louisiana, to a teenaged mother, Jacinda Carter. Dwayne does not remember his father, who abandoned the family by the time Dwayne was two years old. Various sources report Dwayne's father's name as Dwayne Carter or Dwayne Turner. When he was young, Dwayne and his mother lived with his grandmother in the Hollygrove

Because he never knew the father he was named after, Dwayne later decided to drop the *D* from his name and go by Wayne. "He has never been in my life, so I don't want to be Dwayne. I want to be Wayne," he later explained to reporter Katie Couric.[2]

neighborhood of the city's Seventeenth Ward. It is one of the city's poorest neighborhoods, known for its run-down housing, high crime levels, and drug trade.

The tough circumstances Dwayne was born into drove his ambition from an early age. "I always say my city is the reason for my drive, why I'm so motivated to do what I do, because when you're from New Orleans, you gotta do something," he later told cable television network VH1.[1]

MUSICAL ASPIRATIONS

The young Dwayne did well at Lafayette Elementary School, where he qualified for the school's gifted program and performed in the music group Kids with Attitude. His passion and flair for music was evident early on. After writing his first rap at the age of eight, Dwayne started performing everywhere—on the streets, at block parties, and in his grandmother's living room—for anyone who would listen to him. "I was the only child, so whenever anybody came to the house, it was showtime. I couldn't wait," he recalled during an interview with *Rolling Stone* magazine.[3]

Dwayne soon started calling himself Gangsta D and hanging out with Lil Slim, another rapper from the neighborhood. Lil Slim was recording an album through the New Orleans–based label Cash Money Records, and he put Dwayne in touch with Cash Money CEO Bryan "Birdman" Williams and his brother Ron "Slim" Williams in 1991. Bryan Williams recalled meeting young Dwayne when the nine-year-old rapper came to a record signing and spontaneously started performing. Williams immediately thought he had discovered an unusual talent with a lot of potential and gave Dwayne his business card. Dwayne called the number on the card persistently, leaving raps on the Cash Money answering machine. Finally, the Williams brothers started letting him hang around the office doing odd jobs. Bryan Williams took the young rapper under his wing, bringing him to label parties to let him show off for others in the business. The Williams brothers thought it was entertaining to see such a young child rapping about adult subjects such as guns and violence, but they were also grooming Dwayne for his eventual career.

Dwayne didn't have to wait long. He officially signed with Cash Money Records on May 13, 1993, when he was just 11 years old and in sixth grade. The Williams brothers didn't immediately start recording him, but by age 12—under the name Baby D—he was teamed up with 14-year-old

Kim's Supermarket, formerly Solomon's, was one of Dwayne's hangouts in the Hollygrove neighborhood. The market closed after Hurricane Katrina in 2005.

rapper B.G. to form the Baby Gangstaz, or B.G.z. The duo released the album *True Story* in 1995.

Many saw signing with a music label as a way out of the rough life of Hollygrove, where it was common for young children to be drawn into the web of gangs, violence, and drug abuse. But in Dwayne's case, the early taste of success didn't completely save him from the influence of his surroundings. His mother had married a drug dealer, Reginald "Rabbit" McDonald, who became Dwayne's first real father figure and a role model to him. Since Cash Money wasn't paying him much yet, and the money went directly to his mother, Dwayne started dealing marijuana and cocaine to have spending money. He also started dipping into his own stash, becoming a user of illegal drugs at a very young age.

||||||||||||||||||||||||||||||||||||||||||||||||||||||||||||

CLOSE CALL

Dwayne's musical ambitions were almost derailed permanently when he experienced a brush with death at age 11 in 1993. He was home alone watching a music video featuring rapper Notorious B.I.G. while playing with his mother's handgun in front of the mirror. He was under the influence of marijuana. The gun went off, and he accidentally shot himself in the chest. After blacking out, he woke up and dragged himself to a phone to call for help. Then he passed out again until police arrived.

One of the police officers on the scene, known in the neighborhood as Uncle John, later described the incident in an interview with VH1. He recalled arriving at the building and hearing nothing but loud music coming from Dwayne's apartment. Dwayne woke up to the sound of the police pounding on the door. He summoned the strength to pull himself into the living room until he was close enough for them to hear his cries for help. Then the police officers kicked in the door to get to him. "He was drifting in and out of consciousness, his eyes were drifting backward into his head," the officer recalled. "I kept talking to him the whole time (on the way to the hospital), trying to keep him awake . . . trying to keep him alive."[5] At the hospital, doctors found out the bullet had landed just two inches (5 cm) from Dwayne's heart— close enough that they left the bullet fragments in instead of risking surgery to remove them.

The incident scared Dwayne's mother. She had gone to school with the Williams brothers and felt they had a gangster reputation. She responded to Dwayne's irresponsible behavior and slipping grades by forbidding him from spending time at Cash Money Records unless he did better in school. Dwayne took the message to heart and devoted more time to his schoolwork. In middle school, he started attending Eleanor McMain

When he was in seventh grade, Dwayne played a munchkin in his school's production of *The Wiz*. "He didn't always behave, but as far as an actor, you couldn't ask for anything better," said Marta Bivins, his drama teacher at McMain. "He was very talented. He was very committed to his character."[6]

Secondary School, a public magnet school that accepts students from all over New Orleans who are gifted in academics, music, or theater. At McMain, he became involved in his school's theater productions and band, playing cymbals in the percussion section.

Through band, he met Cortez Bryant, who would later become Dwayne's professional manager. Bryant was three years ahead of him in school. He was smart, well spoken, and clean cut. The boys connected when they were the only two members of the cymbals section to show up to practice one day. Back then, Bryant actually discouraged his friend from pursuing a hip-hop career because he didn't think it was a realistic ambition. But Dwayne was determined.

||||||||||

The multitalented Dwayne could act, rap, and play the cymbals.

By the late 1990s, Lil Wayne, *left*, was ready for his career with Cash Money Records and Bryan Williams, *right*, to take off.

CHAPTER 3
Growing Up

O n July 20, 1997, gun violence made its second major appearance in Dwayne's life. That was the day his stepfather was gunned down outside a gas station. Dwayne became the main provider for his family at age 14, taking over bills such as the mortgage and car payment. "Tragedy made me a man," he later recalled.[1]

That was also the year he dropped out of Eleanor McMain Secondary School

Lil Wayne got his first tattoo in memory of his stepfather. It is on his right arm and reads, "In memory of Rabbit: It's up to me."[4]

to fully devote his life to music. He and three other Cash Money rappers—Juvenile, B.G., and Young Turk—formed the Hot Boys, and Dwayne took on the name Lil Wayne for the first time. The Hot Boys' debut album, *Get It How U Live!*, came out in 1997. *Billboard* magazine praised the debut for "parlaying the four Hot Boys' catchy, varied styles into an amusing, if incorrigible, collection of hardcore rap. . . . Though ultimately lacking substance, the Hot Boys' tales will please fans of well-done gangsta rap."[2] *Get It How U Live!* reached Number 37 on the *Billboard* R&B/hip-hop chart and sold more than 400,000 copies.[3]

After receiving his first big paycheck, Lil Wayne gave the money to his mother to buy a new house. He also provided for his daughter, Reginae Carter, who was born on November 28, 1998, shortly after Lil Wayne turned 16. The mother was his 14-year-old girlfriend, Antonia "Toya" Johnson, whom he later married. Although he was young,

Lil Wayne happily took on his new role as a father. "She says I'm the best daddy in the world, but every kid says that," he said later of Reginae. "She's a great kid. She's mine. She's perfectly mine."[5]

Lil Wayne was able to make sure his family was taken care of before his music career took him out of New Orleans for the first time, as the Hot Boys took off on their first tour. The album's success also was good for the Cash Money Records label, which for the first time was in a position to land a deal with Universal Records for national distribution.

||||||||||||||||||||||||||||||||||||||||||||||||||||||||||||||||||

LIKE FAMILY

With his father absent and his stepfather murdered, the Williams brothers became father figures to Lil Wayne. When he was on the road, Ron Williams looked out for him, making sure Lil Wayne rode the same bus as him and stayed in hotel rooms directly next to his. As Lil Wayne later recalled,

> He would always tell me, first and foremost, "You're different from everybody else. You're not a gangster. You're not stupid. We're not going to

Bryan Williams became like another father to Lil Wayne.

have to worry about you getting in trouble with drugs or people trying to kill you." Basically, he was saying, "You're a good kid. Remain a good kid."[6]

Ron noticed how naturally intelligent Lil Wayne was and encouraged him to work hard. "All of us at Cash Money brought him up like that," Ron later recalled. "It's hard in New Orleans—not too many of us make it out. I'm so proud of him, to see him doing these things now and to know where he came from."[7]

||||||||||||||||||||||||||||||||||||||||||||||||||||||||||||||

SOUTHERN SOUND

The Hot Boys followed up their first success with another album, *Guerrilla Warfare*, in 1999. It features the hit singles "I Need a Hot Girl" and "We On Fire." It debuted at Number 1 on the *Billboard* R&B/hip-hop chart and Number 5 on the *Billboard* 200. Within months, it had gone platinum. Critics showered the group's follow-up effort with praise and predicted rising stardom for the four young performers. *Rolling Stone* called the music "inventive," while *Rap Pages* used the words "phenomenal" and "nearly flawless." The *Source*, another music magazine, said the quartet had given "southern bounce an artistic shot in the arm."[8]

GROWING UP ON THE ROAD ||||||||||||||||||||||||||||||||||||||||||||||||

Signing with Cash Money and becoming a rap star at an early age meant Lil Wayne did not have a normal adolescence. "I grew up on the road," he once said. "I grew up in the clubs, at the bank, in the office, in the studio. I grew up in New York, running up on Universal. I grew up in L.A. at Universal Sheraton."[9]

Bounce refers to an energetic style of hip-hop that was born in New Orleans. It's party music, with generally lighthearted lyrics rapped over samples of dance beats. One major component of the style is the use of repetitive call-and-response lyrics to get an audience involved. In the 1990s, Cash Money Records became known for its signature bounce style of hip-hop through the talents of Mannie Fresh, who produced the Hot Boys' albums. While some in the hip-hop world didn't view it as authentic rap music, Fresh argued there is a valid place for fun in the genre. "It's a whole planet full of people out there, and being hard is not everybody's thing," Fresh said. "Most people just want to have a good time."[10]

NEW ORLEANS ROOTS

In an interview with *Rolling Stone*, Lil Wayne described how growing up in New Orleans influenced his music: "You can't listen to most New Orleans music and listen to mine and compare, they're so different. But how New Orleans is in my music is, we have this drive about us. We have this motivation. You see people on the corner, singing, and that takes a different type of pride to do that. . . . But music, rap music I think that's where New Orleans comes in. We're relentless when it comes to music."[11]

Lil Wayne's career took off with the Hot Boys, *clockwise from top left*: Lil Wayne, Young Turk, B.G., and Juvenile.

While pure bounce music tends to be too explicit to be played on the radio or put on a studio album, the breakout success of the Hot Boys proved there was definitely a market for rap artists with a background in bounce. After becoming known as a bounce artist, Lil Wayne was ready to put his unique spin on the sound and make a name for himself as a solo performer.

Lil Wayne's solo music has always stayed true to himself.

CHAPTER 4
Breaking Out

||||||||||||||||||||||||||||||||||||||||||||||||||||||||||||||||||||||||||

I n 1999, the same year the Hot Boys released *Guerrilla Warfare*, Lil Wayne released his first solo album. By that point, fellow Hot Boys Juvenile and B.G. had already put out several solo albums each, and the younger Lil Wayne was eager to catch up.

Lil Wayne started working on the material when he was 14. He considers that first solo work to be the time when he started finding his own voice and setting himself apart from the other group members. "You got to find yourself in life, period," he told MTV. "I always tell people the only thing that makes my raps good is 'cause I rap about what I am. I got reality rap."[1]

Instead of focusing on what would sell and make the most money—or "bling bling," as Lil Wayne would say—he just wanted to make what he thought was good music. From the beginning, Bryan Williams backed up Lil Wayne and others on this philosophy, giving his young Cash Money artists the freedom to produce the music they wanted and trusting their talent and hard work would pay off.

This strategy worked for Lil Wayne. Released on November 2, 1999, *Tha Block Is Hot* debuted at Number 1 on the *Billboard* R&B/hip-hop chart and Number 3 on the *Billboard* 200. More than 200,000 copies sold during the album's first week,

SLANG SLINGER

Lil Wayne has been credited with coining or popularizing several slang phrases, including "drop it like it's hot" and "bling." He was the one who added the lyric "drop it like it's hot" on a hit single by Juvenile. He also came up with the word "bling" to use on a song of B.G.'s that came to be called "Bling Bling."

One thing that set apart Lil Wayne's debut album, *Tha Block Is Hot*, from the work of other rappers was that he did not use curse words on it. He reportedly kept the language relatively clean to make his mother happy. However, the Recording Industry Association of America (RIAA) still required a parental advisory label for mature subject matters such as sex and violence. Beginning with *Lights Out*, Lil Wayne started using the foul language typical of most rap music.

and it topped 1 million sales several months later.[2] Lil Wayne thanked his fans after going platinum. "I appreciate that. So now I'm soaking in the success of being young and . . . having the hottest car," he said.[3] The promise shown in his debut also earned him a Source Awards nomination for Best New Artist in 2000.

MATURING SOUND

Lil Wayne followed up his debut album one year later with the release of *Lights Out* on December 19, 2000. In his early solo work, critics started noticing Lil Wayne's tendency to combine the fun beats reminiscent of his Hot Boys days with more interesting lyrics. A reviewer at *Allmusic* noted the more substantial tone of *Lights Out* was "dropping serious lyrics over Mannie Fresh's wildest production to date."[4] *Lights Out* includes the songs "Everything," which honors Lil Wayne's stepfather, and "Grown Man," in which Lil Wayne contemplates his growing adult responsibilities. "The album's subject matter . . . is hardly novel, but Wayne imbues his work with a sense of boyish enthusiasm that keeps matters from getting too grim, in the process capturing the . . . [feeling] of Cash Money's best work," an *AV Club* reviewer wrote.[5]

By 2002, B.G. and Juvenile were leaving Cash Money Records after disputes concerning money, leaving the label in a difficult financial position. The pressure was on Lil Wayne to sustain the label, and he stepped up to the challenge with his third album in three years. Called *500 Degreez*, the album appeared to be an attempt to top Juvenile's third album, which had been titled *400 Degreez* and had been Cash Money's best-selling album to date. But Lil Wayne insisted in interviews there were no hard feelings at the label toward the rappers who left. He expressed hope his third studio effort would show how he was growing up and highlight the new experiences he'd had since touring outside of New Orleans. The 21-track album was released on July 23, 2002, and sold just under 1 million copies.[6]

Although his second and third albums were hits, they did not sell as well as *Tha Block Is Hot*, and some critics felt he had not done enough yet to set himself apart from his fellow Hot Boys. *USA Today* reviewer Steve Jones wrote that Lil Wayne had not succeeded in his attempt to top Juvenile with *500 Degreez*. "Wayne covers too much of the same bling-bling and gangsta territory that has been trodden so many times before," Jones wrote. "Wayne may well be rhyming about the lifestyle he knows, but he needs a fresh perspective to go along with that [Mannie] Fresh production."[7] Some wondered if the promising young star would live

NICKNAMES

When he launched his solo career, Lil Wayne started going by another nickname—Weezy F. Baby. The name referred to his famously raspy voice. Other nicknames he has used over the years include Birdman Jr., Dr. Carter, Gangsta D, Mr. Carter, Shrimp Daddy, President Carter, Rapper Eater, Tune, Tunechi Lionchess, Nino Brown, and Wizzle.

Since the beginning of his solo career, Lil Wayne has been more interested in the music than the bling.

up to his potential. Others thought if Cash Money Records didn't come up with a new strategy soon, the once-hot label might be on its way out.

|||||||||||

Lil Wayne has always been
confident in himself and his music.

CHAPTER 5

Breakthrough

||||||||||||||||||||||||||||||||||||||||||||||||||||||||||||||||||||||||||||||||||||||

With Cash Money Records struggling, stakes were high for Lil Wayne's next album to be a bigger success than his previous outings. But instead of weighing him down, the pressure fed into the young rapper's competitive spirit. He felt confident *Tha Carter*—his fourth album by age 20—would put a stop to any talk of Cash Money fading away while putting him back on top of the charts where he thought he belonged. "It's a new me, older me," Lil Wayne told an interviewer. "My people feel like this album will make people go 'he is not just a rapper, he's one of the best.'"[1]

> **"When we started, [Bryan Williams] told us at the time that what the East Coast is doing is fine, what the West Coast is doing is fine, but now we're gonna bring the South to it. And it blew up. It's blowing up."[2]**
>
> *—LIL WAYNE*

The songs covered more personal topics such as what it was like to be a teenage father and to experience such early success. He also spent time reminiscing about his surrogate family members at Cash Money Records—letting himself be more sentimental than is usually typical of rap music. Mannie Fresh stayed on as producer, incorporating his own flavor while also tailoring the beats to Lil Wayne's style. It would be the last album Fresh produced for the label.

In preparation for the much-anticipated album, Lil Wayne released the first of a series of mixtapes—*Da Drought* and *Da Drought 2*—as a way to promote himself. "He wanted to communicate with his fans directly to build his brand," explained music writer Ben Westhoff. "His mixtapes were his way of getting around the media idiots who didn't appreciate him properly."[3] Instead of being sold, the mixtapes were sent to clubs and radio stations. In the meantime, the album's release date was pushed back.

Lil Wayne also starting signing artists under his own label, which came to be called Young Money Entertainment, begun in 2003. It was to be run under the umbrella of the existing Cash Money and Universal Records partnership. The label's first artists included Squad Up (a group that included

MARRIAGE |||||||||||||||||||||||||||||||||||||||||||||||||||||||||||||||||||||||||||||||||||||||||||||||||||||

The same year *Tha Carter* came out, Lil Wayne married Antonia "Toya" Johnson, who had been his girlfriend since middle school. He first proposed to her approximately two years after their daughter, Reginae, was born, when Lil Wayne was 17 and Toya was 16 years old. She finally accepted his proposal when they were 21 and 20 years old, respectively. They got married on Valentine's Day in 2004.

They decided to divorce in 2006, after their marriage had difficulties from Lil Wayne's time on the road. They have stayed on good terms to continue raising their daughter together.

Lil Wayne), New Orleans native rapper Gutter Gutter, and the R&B group Real.

||||||||||||||||||||||||||||||||||||||||||||||||||

THA CARTER

Tha Carter finally hit stores on June 29, 2004. It features Lil Wayne's biggest hit to date, a single called "Go DJ," which went to Number 14 on the *Billboard* Hot 100. The catchy refrains made it hugely popular in clubs around the country. More than 100,000 copies of the album sold in the first week.[4] It debuted in the Number 5 slot on the *Billboard* 200.

Perhaps more telling than the numbers, critics heaped praise on the album as a big step forward for Lil Wayne. A *New York Times* reviewer wrote that with the beginning of the Tha Carter series, Lil Wayne had finally broken free of the more restrictive rhyme patterns left over from his Hot Boys days. "His phrasing has grown looser, trickier, and funnier," the reviewer wrote.[5]

As he became more established as a solo performer, Lil Wayne became known for his trademark colorful wordplay. His lyrics feature a variety of imagery, similes, and metaphors. Entire Web sites are devoted to celebrating his punning and poeticizing. But surprisingly, Lil Wayne never writes down his lyrics before going into the recording studio. Lil Wayne stopped writing down lyrics when he was 16. He does carry a notebook with him and occasionally jots down ideas in it. When recording music for an album, he sometimes goes into the studio with a concept or vague idea of what he wants to record and then improvises the lyrics on the spot. But more often, he uses whatever happens to be in his head at the moment. On how he comes up with his lyrics, he said,

> I think you as a listener have to word it as "lyrics,"
> but me, I'm just being me. It's not "lyrics," so I

SIGNATURE STYLE

By the time he released *Tha Carter*, Lil Wayne was wearing his hair in dreadlocks, a look that has become something of a trademark for him. He has also become known for the dozens of tattoos he has covering his body, which he has said describe various aspects of his life. They include teardrops on his cheeks, Jay Z lyrics on his leg, a large wing on the side of his chest, his hometown area code on his arm, a smiley face on the inside of his lip, and many more. Another striking aspect of his appearance is his teeth, which have been plated in metal and diamonds.

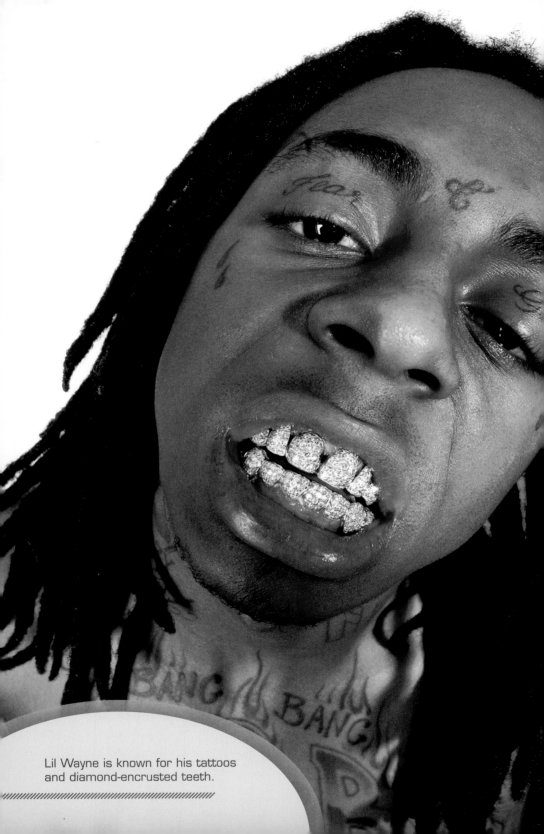

Lil Wayne is known for his tattoos
and diamond-encrusted teeth.

don't have to come up with it. . . . When you write, you live within that paper and then you're only as good as your last line. So I don't write, I don't have a last line. I'm just trying to get better.[6]

LOYALTY AND OPPORTUNITIES

With the success of *Tha Carter*, other labels started trying to pull Lil Wayne away from Cash Money Records. In response, Bryan Williams promoted the young rapper to company president. As president, Lil Wayne would be more involved in shaping new artists who signed with Cash Money. He would have a say in everything from their music to their look.

Lil Wayne also felt very loyal to the Williams brothers for all they had done for him. He stayed put and went back to the studio to crank out his next album, *Tha Carter II*.

Hurricane Katrina caused widespread flooding, loss of life, and other damage in New Orleans.

CHAPTER 6

Rebuilding and Respect

||||||||||||||||||||||||||||||||||||||||||||||||||||||||||||||||||||||||||||||||||

J ust as Cash Money was rebuilding, it experienced another huge blow—one that was felt throughout New Orleans and the surrounding areas. Hurricane Katrina struck on August 29, 2005, flooding large portions of the city and resulting in the loss of more than 1,800 lives. Bryan Williams told CBS News he lost $20 million in assets, including multiple residences, cars, and the Cash Money headquarters. The sentimental value of what was lost was also high. "You come from nothing to something, and you feel like you accomplish something and we got a little head start and out the 'hood. To see you lose everything—if I wasn't strong, I would have folded."[1] He went on to acknowledge that while he had money to fall back on and start over, many Katrina victims were not as lucky.

Lil Wayne and his family members were out of town when the storm struck, but his old Hollygrove neighborhood—in the low-lying Seventeenth Ward—was largely destroyed by the severe flooding. During several of his later recordings, Lil Wayne criticized the government's response to the disaster and levee system that failed. On a 2006 mixtape, for example, he rapped, "So what happened to the levees? Why wasn't they steady?"[2]

DEMANDING RESPECT

With much of the city underwater, Lil Wayne and Cash Money Records moved to Miami, Florida. Although they had changed location, they

Lil Wayne's success meant Cash Money Records was becoming a bigger player in the music world.

remained committed to preserving the particular style of hip-hop that had originated in New Orleans and been popularized largely by Cash Money Records. Lil Wayne told the Associated Press southern hip-hop was on the scene to stay. He complained hip-hop artists from the rest of the country were getting an unfair amount of attention while southern rappers were being disrespected. This was a theme that appeared on his fifth album,

> "I just always expect the best because I'm a competitor and if I'm competing, then obviously I'm trying to be better in everything. I have no challengers—the challenger is everything—so I try to be the best."[4]
>
> —LIL WAYNE

Tha Carter II. On the track "Shooter," he rapped, "To the radio stations, I'm tired of being patient / Stop being rapper racist, region-haters. . . . This is Southern; face it."[3]

While *Tha Carter* had been successful, *Tha Carter II* further cemented Lil Wayne's stardom and propped up the Cash Money label for the foreseeable future. With a lineup of new producers to replace the departed Fresh, Lil Wayne dazzled music critics and fans alike. "These guys have chewed up reggae and blues and metal and spit them back out as diamond-hard unforgiving Southern smash-rock or as gorgeous glistening East Coast cinematic soul-rap," wrote a *Village Voice* reviewer who called "Shooter" the song of the year. "Wayne takes these beats, tracks that few rappers would know what to do with, and he toys with them like a bored cat with a mouse. It's really something."[5] An editorial review from online music store iTunes was similarly glowing:

> Wayne had always maintained a unique style, and had made memorable, even classic recordings in years past, but Tha Carter II broke the mold. Suddenly Wayne was taking risks in his rhymes, experimenting with his voice and his [rhythms], using stream-of-consciousness wordplay that was at times [biting], at times incomprehensible, but never less than stimulating.[6]

Billboard magazine praised Lil Wayne for taking risks on the album while also staying true to his roots: "Birdman and Slim [Williams] knew something everyone else didn't when they bet the farm on the formerly 'raw talent,' not 'fully formed' Lil Wayne."[7]

FAMILY EFFORT

Lil Wayne felt Cash Money Records was more his home than his workplace. In tribute to their bond, he and Bryan Williams collaborated on an album called *Like Father, Like Son*. Released in 2006, the album did well, debuting at Number 3 on the *Billboard* 200. "It's a great turning point for us in the game," Williams said afterward. "What we did last year was just the beginning."[8]

While he was prone to boasting about his own talent, in more serious interviews, Lil Wayne talked about the hard work that went into making each finished product. "We don't approach things like, 'we're good,'" he told reporter Katie Couric. "We approach things like we're going to work and going to work hard. And if you work hard, you get good."[9] The work ethic he applied during the making of *Tha Carter II* paid off. After its release on December 5, 2005, the album quickly defied projections, selling 238,000 copies in one week and eventually going platinum. It debuted at Number 2 on the *Billboard* 200 and at Number 1 on both the *Billboard* R&B/hip-hop and rap albums charts. It was easily the highest-selling album in Cash Money history.

Within days of the album's release, Lil Wayne received more good news. Earlier that year, he had collaborated with Destiny's Child and T.I. on the song "Soldier." On December 8, 2005, they learned they had been nominated for a Grammy Award in the Best Rap/Sung Collaboration category. It was the 23-year-old rapper's first Grammy nomination.

||||||||||||||||||||||||||||||||||||||||||||||||||||||||

MAINSTREAM SUCCESS

Lil Wayne had finally reached the level of fame where he was well known outside of the hip-hop world. He didn't release his next album, *Tha Carter III*, for more than two years, but his name, face, and music still seemed to be almost everywhere. He was releasing massive amounts of music on mixtapes and doing numerous appearances on other artists' tracks and videos. He worked with Usher, Ja Rule, T-Pain, Electric Red, Shakira, Fall Out Boy, Enrique Iglesias, Beyoncé, and many others, drawing in at least $100,000 for each spot. "Everybody is always sending me something, and I never say no," he said.[11]

When he finally did release the widely anticipated *Tha Carter III* in June 2008, it sold more than 1 million copies in its first week. It included the hit single "Lollipop," which was

Lil Wayne made his second appearance on *Saturday Night Live* in 2010 with rapper Eminem.

downloaded more than 2 million times.[12] The song also led to Lil Wayne's first time taking the top spot in the *Billboard* Hot 100. "Lollipop" was written for a late friend, R&B artist Steve "Static Major"

Garrett. Other songs on the album paid tribute to New Orleans in the wake of Hurricane Katrina.

Rolling Stone music reviewer Jody Rosen wrote the album confirmed Lil Wayne really was the "best rapper alive," as he often liked to claim. "It establishes beyond a doubt that the [cultural spirit] in 2008 belongs to one artist: a dreadlocked . . . poet from New Orleans with . . . a voice like a bullfrog," Rosen wrote. "As Wayne croaks in the woozy '3 Peat,' 'Get on my level / You can't get on my level / You will need a space shuttle / Or a ladder that's forever.'"[13]

||||||||||||

EXPOSURE |||||||||||||||||||||||||||||||||||||||||||||||||||||||||||||||||||||||||||||||||||||||||||||||||||||||||||||||||||||||

As Lil Wayne gained more mainstream popularity, he started making appearances in prime time. He appeared on the television comedy *Saturday Night Live* for the first time in 2008 and was asked to return in 2010. He was interviewed on *Jimmy Kimmel Live* in 2009.

Lil Wayne accepted four Grammy Awards on February 8, 2009.

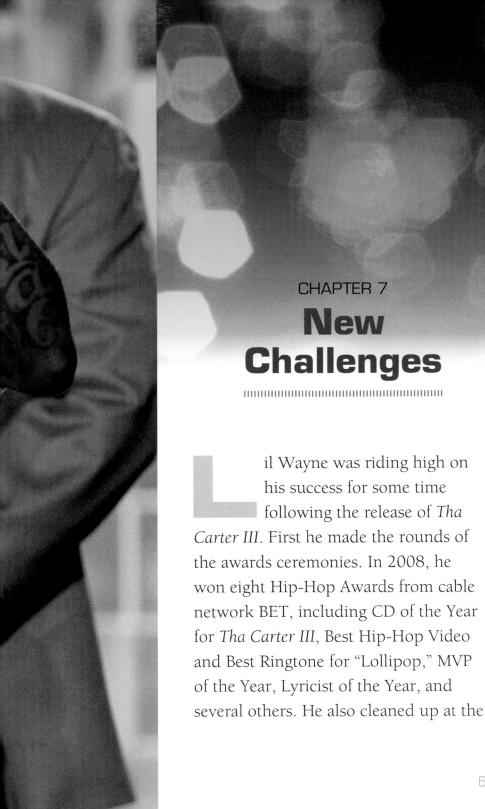

CHAPTER 7

New Challenges

IIIIIIIIIIIIIIIIIIIIIIIIIIIIIIIIIIIIIIIIIIIIIIIIIIIIIIIIIIIIII

il Wayne was riding high on his success for some time following the release of *Tha Carter III*. First he made the rounds of the awards ceremonies. In 2008, he won eight Hip-Hop Awards from cable network BET, including CD of the Year for *Tha Carter III*, Best Hip-Hop Video and Best Ringtone for "Lollipop," MVP of the Year, Lyricist of the Year, and several others. He also cleaned up at the

2009 Grammy Awards, winning Best Rap Song for "Lollipop," Best Rap Performance by a Group for "Swagga Like Us," Best Rap Album for *Tha Carter III*, and Best Solo Performance for "A Milli." Also in 2009, he won Songwriter of the Year from the BMI music company Urban Music Awards and Best Male Hip-Hop Artist from the BET Awards. He performed at the 2009 Grammy Awards, paying tribute to his hometown of New Orleans with a performance of the song "Tie My Hands."

His popularity was even spreading internationally, and he took his first tour through Europe. Lil Wayne was overwhelmed by the warm reception after his European fans seemed to know all the words to his songs and greeted him so enthusiastically. "It's one thing to say you're hot in your city, your state, your region," he said. "But when you step out of the country and they scream your name—I don't know if that's good for my ego. I'm very surprised."[1]

While his own career was hopping, he was also working on getting the careers of several other artists going through his label Young Money Entertainment. His protégés included Nicki Minaj and Drake, whom he promoted through

Lil Wayne recognized and promoted the talent of up-and-comers Nicki Minaj, *center*, and Drake, *left*.

appearances on mixtapes and in music videos. To introduce them and the rest of his Young Money crew to the world, in 2009 he launched a tour called Young Money Presents: The America's Most Wanted Music Tour. On the tour, Lil Wayne headlined, performing his usual hip-hop routine along with some new rock sounds he had started experimenting with.

Lil Wayne's personal life was also eventful during this time. On October 22, 2008, Lil

Drake, who has sold millions of albums and won a Grammy, credits Lil Wayne for signing him to Young Money and taking him under his wing. As the Williams brothers had done for him, Lil Wayne likes to give his protégés space to develop their own styles. "He doesn't give his input on how we should be, or how we should rap, or how we should dress. Wayne just gives us the opportunity," Drake said.[2] Nicki Minaj said she appreciated how involved Lil Wayne was in promoting the artists at his label. "I don't think people know how smart he is. He's a thinker. People think he's just doing records. He has a plan for everything."[3]

Wayne's first son, Dwayne Michael Carter III, was born in Cincinnati, Ohio, to Sarah Vivian. Less than a year later, he and actress Laura London welcomed another baby boy, Cameron Carter, who was born on September 9, 2009. Another girlfriend, pop singer Nivea, also had a son with Lil Wayne—Neal Carter—born on November 30, 2009.

REBIRTH

After reaching the top of the hip-hop world, Lil Wayne decided it was time to push himself in a new direction. He started work on a rock album, his seventh studio album, which he would call *Rebirth*. The effort required him to work on skills he hadn't used much before, such as playing guitar and singing. "The *Rebirth* album is just me expressing myself without any boundaries. Without any margins, without any guidelines," Lil Wayne told MTV. "I'm trying to do something different."[4]

There was a lot of skepticism regarding the rumor that Lil Wayne was putting out a rock album. A lot of people assumed it was going to have his usual hip-hop sound, only with a little guitar and some extra drumbeats thrown in. One of Lil Wayne's producers, Infamous, who produced the album's hit single "Prom Queen," admitted in an interview he had assumed that before going into the studio. But when they started working, Lil Wayne incorporated a full rock band's worth of instruments—guitar, bass, and drums—while saying no to synthesizers. "That's when I realized it was actually going to be a real rock album," Infamous told *Billboard*. "He's done everything he can with hip-hop and has proven himself. Now he's about to prove himself as a rocker and we're excited to be a part of it."[5] As usually happened, parts of the album were leaked ahead of its release, so Lil Wayne added extra tracks at the last minute to keep it fresh.

Originally slated for release in spring 2009, the album finally dropped on February 2, 2010. Reviews were less than positive, but some critics at least admired the artist for what he had wanted to do. A *New York Times* reviewer lamented that Lil Wayne had traded away the most interesting aspects of his music—like the clever wordplay and rapid-fire delivery—for auto-tuned melodies and inexpert guitar riffs. *Entertainment Weekly* compared it to NBA star Michael Jordan's attempt to play professional baseball. Other critics dismissed the effort. *Washington Post* reviewer Allison Stewart didn't pull any punches, calling the album just plain awful:

> *Even as some kind of ironic, post-rap performance art piece, it stinks to high heaven. Worse than how it sounds, though, is what it does: It takes the best . . . rapper in the world and . . . reduces him to an uncertain-sounding amateur on Van Halen karaoke night. The first time you hear "Rebirth" you won't think, "Wow, Weezy sure*

Lil Wayne's foray into rock and playing the guitar was
not well received.

*sounds different." You'll think: "What is Lenny
Kravitz doing to that terrible Korn song?"*[6]

Due to the general buzz that surrounded the
star, however, *Rebirth* still sold fairly well, although
the numbers paled in comparison to megahit
Tha Carter III. Rebirth debuted at Number 2 on
the *Billboard* 200 and sold 176,000 copies in its

A moviemaker who filmed Lil Wayne for the documentary *Tha Carter* recalled the surprising work ethic of the young rap star. "He's like a tireless worker, and a lot of people will be very surprised how he's 100 percent dedicated to his craft. . . . I really gained a lot of respect for him in that regard in terms of how he approaches his records and then how hard he works."[8]

first week.[7] Luckily for fans, though, Lil Wayne's conversion to rock star wasn't permanent, and he had a few more hip-hop albums coming down the pike. Unfortunately, they would have to wait while the rapper got his personal life sorted out.

||||||||||||||||||||||||||||||||||||||||||||||||||

SUBSTANCE ABUSE

Even as Lil Wayne seemed to be at the pinnacle of his career, chronic substance abuse problems and a wild lifestyle were taking their toll behind the scenes. For years, he had been addicted to promethazine-codeine, a type of cough syrup, known by the street name purple drank. He was rarely seen without a cup of the purple liquid. Lil Wayne also had been smoking large amounts of marijuana since picking up the habit as a kid back in Hollygrove. He reportedly only used recording studios or stayed in hotels that allowed him to smoke marijuana while there.

Even as his popularity soared and his albums were topping charts, cover stories focused on the potential cost of the hip-hop legend's wild lifestyle. Some even predicted he was headed toward an early death. But during this time, Lil Wayne refused to admit his substance abuse problems, instead laughing off the idea that he was an addict:

I'm a very successful addict. And a very smart one. And a very charismatic one. And one that

PURPLE DRANK

Purple drank is a highly addictive mixture of promethazine-codeine cold medication and soda such as Sprite or Mountain Dew. Sipping the mixture causes feelings of happiness and being disconnected from one's body, lasting between three and six hours. Side effects can include slowed heart rate, drowsiness, raspy voice, loss of balance and coordination, uncontrolled eye movement, and dental problems.

Additionally, overdosing on the codeine in purple drank can lead to death. Abuse of purple drank is common in the rapping world and among pro athletes. At least three hip-hop artists and producers are known to have died from overdoses, including DJ Screw, Big Hawk, and Pimp C.

just won four Grammys, and one that sold a million records in a week. One that still appears on everybody's songs, one that still sounds better than any rapper rapping. One that has four kids and is the greatest father ever to the kids. What am I addicted to, being great?[9]

As it turned out, the thing that put a stop to his wild ways—at least temporarily—wasn't an overdose or time in a drug rehabilitation facility. It was a series of run-ins with the law. In 2006, employees at a hotel where Lil Wayne was staying had reported the smell of marijuana coming from the rapper's room. Officers at the scene found marijuana and prescription drugs.

Before those charges were settled, he was charged with something more serious. In 2007, New York City police officers had pulled over Lil Wayne's tour bus after smelling marijuana. They found a .40 caliber handgun on board, which the rapper possessed illegally, along with marijuana, cocaine, and ecstasy. Lil Wayne was charged with weapons misconduct, felony possession of a narcotic drug, possession of dangerous drugs, and possession of drug equipment. After battling the charges for two years while continuing to tour and

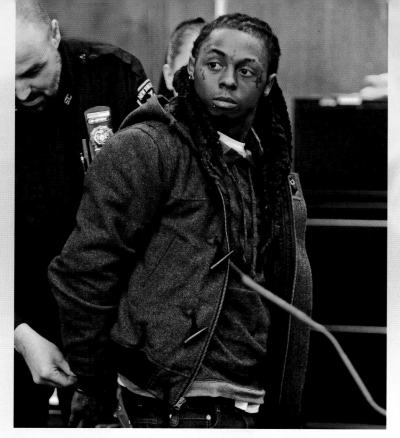

Lil Wayne was sentenced to one year in prison on March 8, 2010.

make music, Lil Wayne reached a plea agreement. He pled guilty to a charge of second-degree attempted criminal possession of a weapon and was sentenced to one year in prison.

||||||||||

Lil Wayne's time in prison forced him to take a break from partying and round-the-clock production work.

CHAPTER 8

On the Inside

||||||||||||||||||||||||||||||||||||||||||||||||||||||||||||||||||||||||||||||||||||||||

The 27-year-old rap phenom began serving his sentence at Rikers Island on February 9, 2010, one week after the release of *Rebirth*. "This is not something you get no advice on," Lil Wayne told a *Rolling Stone* reporter shortly before starting the sentence. "This is Lil Wayne going to jail. Nobody I can talk to can tell me what that's like. I just say I'm looking forward to it."[1]

RELIGIOUS SIDE

While many of his fans may not think of Lil Wayne as a religious person, he considers himself a Christian. He wears a small cross around his neck and has the word *fear* tattooed on one eyelid and *God* tattooed on the other. When he served time in jail, he considered it something God meant for him to do.

Giving up the drugs, the alcohol, and the partying lifestyle was difficult, but perhaps not as difficult as giving up his breakneck production schedule. But the time inside also could have potentially brought something else to a screeching halt—Lil Wayne's larger-than-life stardom. "You can't deny that in this industry, if you sit out six months you'll kill your career," said his manager, Cortez Bryant.[2] Lil Wayne and his crew spent the months leading up to his incarceration preparing. In addition to getting *Rebirth* ready to release, they shot music videos of Lil Wayne's Young Money protégés and recorded tracks with other artists to be released during his sentence. They also launched a Web site through which Lil Wayne could keep in touch with his fans. Plans were made to hype the upcoming album *Tha Carter IV*, which was scheduled to come out shortly after his release.

His colleagues at Young Money Entertainment temporarily moved to New York to stay close to him.

While at Rikers, Carter was kept mostly apart from the rest of the prison population, spending up to eight hours a day with a small number of fellow inmates due to safety concerns because he was a celebrity. In prison, he continued his efforts to stay in the game, writing down lyrics, listening to the radio, and even rapping over the phone while his producers recorded him. He stayed in touch with his colleagues to keep up with what was going on in the industry and read fan mail, even personally answering some of the letters. Artists including Kanye West and Nicki Minaj stopped by to visit. His manager even thought the experience—and the extra time to reflect on his life—could be beneficial to Lil Wayne's music. In the meantime, Lil Wayne

SOLITARY CONFINEMENT

Several months into his sentence, Lil Wayne was caught with an MP3 player and headphones, which one of his visitors had slipped to him. The items were confiscated, and he spent a month in solitary confinement for the infraction. During this time he was allowed to interact with other inmates for just one hour per day.

stayed in the public's eye through new releases such as the song "Right Above It," featuring Drake, and "No Love," his collaboration with rapper Eminem. His label also stayed active, releasing debut albums for Drake and Nicki Minaj, as well as a Young Money compilation.

||||||||||||||||||||||||||||||||||||||||||||||||||||||||||||||||

NEW RELEASE

On September 27, 2010—the rapper's twenty-eighth birthday—Lil Wayne's album of prerecorded material *I Am Not a Human Being* was released. From prison, he issued the following statement to his fans: "I want to give a gift on my birthday to my loyal fans who have continued to support me."[3] The album was a return to his hip-hop roots and was much better received than his brief venture into rock had been. While he had rushed to complete the recordings before going to prison, critics noted the material did not feel rushed and showed no signs the rapper was facing incarceration while working on it. "In Wayne's patented way, the songs feel tossed-off: He has a gift for making [great skill] sound casual, while delivering laugh-out-loud punch lines every few

In an interview, Lil Wayne explained the meaning of the album title *I Am Not a Human Being*, which was released during his time in prison: "It's just saying that I'm not the same as other people. I don't think the same. I don't do the same things. I just feel out of this world sometimes."[5]

seconds," wrote a *Rolling Stone* reviewer. "You won't hear a funnier record all year. Jailbird or civilian, human or moon man, Lil Wayne is pop's most reliable deliverer of unadulterated fun. He's also the greatest rapper alive."[4]

It reached the Number 1 slot on the *Billboard* 200, which made Lil Wayne only the second artist to achieve the feat while incarcerated (rapper Tupac Shakur was the first). It reached platinum status by the end of 2010.

||||||||||||||||||||||||||||||||||||||||||||||||||||||||||

FREE AT LAST

After receiving time off for good behavior, Lil Wayne was released on November 4, 2010. Ready to throw himself full blast back into the music business, he made plans to start recording

Lil Wayne was excited to be reunited with his family, including children Reginae and Dwayne Michael Carter III.

on a private plane on the way to see his family. Fans were excited to have Lil Wayne back in the studio. Even after two album releases in one year, anticipation was building for the fourth installment in the Tha Carter series.

Originally slated to be released shortly after his prison sentence ended, *Tha Carter IV* was pushed back to 2011. Lil Wayne said he came up with a lot of new material while he was behind bars, and he spent months after his release perfecting it. Bryan Williams joked that the biggest problem finishing the album was simply deciding what to put on it, since Lil Wayne had generated so much music since the last Carter album.

In the meantime, his first single off the album, "6 Foot 7 Foot," was well received. "What's really reassuring about '6 Foot 7 Foot' is how familiar it sounds," wrote a *New York Times* critic. "It sounds like Wayne just before he went away."[6] While the album has its lighter moments, many of the tracks show what Lil Wayne thought about while he had so much time to himself, with mortality and clocks as repeated themes. When the album was released on August 29, it sold more than 964,000 copies in its first week, debuting at Number 1 on the *Billboard* 200.[7] It was the biggest debut of any hip-hop album since *Tha Carter III* in 2008.

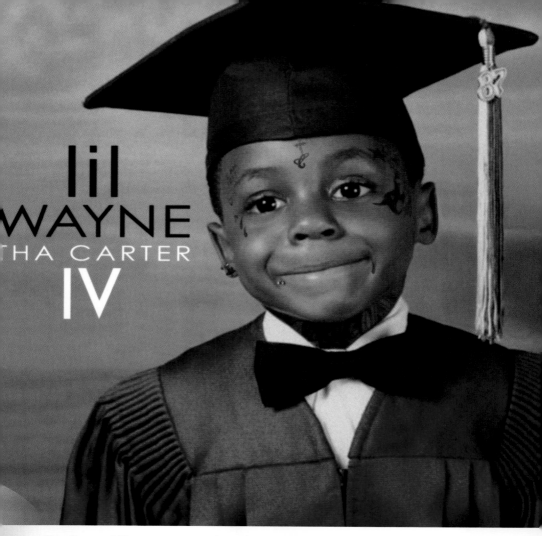

lil
WAYNE
THA CARTER
IV

Tha Carter IV features guest spots from Drake, rapper T-Pain, singer John Legend, and many others.

The number seemed to prove the time away had not diminished Lil Wayne's popularity.

Many reviewers thought the album was uneven, however. *Rolling Stone* gave it three and a half out of five stars. The reviewer wrote that even the parts of the album that weren't great were at least distinctly Lil Wayne, showing off his wild personality. Other reviewers thought it fell short of his earlier work. "At his best, Wayne was positively psychedelic in his wordplay, capable of creating entire alternative worlds out of a few surrealist metaphors. But he sounds slower, more methodical, less unhinged on *Tha Carter IV*," wrote a *Chicago Tribune* reviewer.[8]

|||||||||||

I Am Not a Human Being 2 was one of the most anticipated albums of 2013, but many felt it fell flat.

CHAPTER 9

New Pursuits

|||||||||||||||||||||||||||||||||||||||||||||||||||||||||||||||||||||||||||||

F ollowing *Tha Carter IV*, Lil
Wayne went back to the
studio to work on sequels for
I Am Not a Human Being, *Rebirth*, and
Like Father, Like Son, the album he had
collaborated on with Bryan Williams
in 2006. *I Am Not a Human Being 2*,
Lil Wayne's tenth solo album, came
out on March 26, 2013, debuting at
Number 2 on the *Billboard* 200. It was
met with a lukewarm reception, as Lil
Wayne seemed to be finding it harder

Lil Wayne helped launch the Trukfit brand on June 1, 2012.

and harder to meet sky-high expectations and top his own work. However, his critical success continued with multiple awards, including the 2011 BET Hip-Hop Award for Best Lyricist and the 2012 *Billboard* Music Awards Top Male Artist.

After releasing his tenth album, Lil Wayne started what would be a 40-city tour with artists T.I. and Future. And he continued to look after his Young Money crew. In addition to the artists' albums and collaborations, the label branched out to offer a prepaid debit card and three clothing lines by 2012, including the skater clothing brand Trukfit at Macy's department stores. The avid sports fan even became a blogger for cable sports network ESPN.

Making time for his family of four children has always been a priority for Lil Wayne. He takes great pride in being able to provide for his children and enjoys spending time with each of them. His oldest daughter, Reginae, once gave an interview in which she revealed her rap star father helps her with her school projects and sometimes lets her travel the world with him. Taking after her dad with a flair for music, Reginae has even started her own music group, the OMG Girlz. In one of her songs, she raps, "They love me and they hate me cuz I'm Weezy F's daughter . . . And I'm stuntin' like my daddy cuz I'm daddy's little girl."[1]

|||||||||||||||||||||||||||||||||||||||||||||||||||||||

CONTROVERSY

In February 2013, Lil Wayne was in the news when a lyric he wrote upset the family of Emmett

Lil Wayne has said his ability to surprise people and take risks have helped him be successful. "I can explain me in one word: unexplainable. Anybody who can be explained should be ashamed of themselves. I wasn't created, I wasn't made. I was put here and there's no word for it. I can't explain myself. You look at me and tell me what you see, you listen to me and tell me what you get. That's what it is, that's who I am. I am music, ya dig?"[2]

Till, a figure in the American civil rights movement of the mid-1900s. Till, a 14-year-old boy who was black, was beaten and murdered in 1955 after two white men thought he whistled at a white woman. Images of Till's brutally beaten body increased national awareness of racially charged violence. Wayne made a vulgar reference to the teen's death in a remix of hip-hop artist Future's song "Karate Chop." Epic Records said the remix was unauthorized and immediately pulled it from the Internet, and the reference was removed from a future release of the song. Also as a result of the incident, PepsiCo severed ties with Lil Wayne, who previously had a deal to promote Mountain Dew. The company's statement explained the "offensive reference to a revered civil rights icon does not reflect the values of our brand."[3]

In May 2013, Lil Wayne issued a letter to the family. He supported Epic Records' decision to remove the lyric and promised to avoid referencing Till in his future music. "I have tremendous respect for those who paved the way for the liberty and opportunities that African-Americans currently enjoy," he wrote. "As a business owner who employs several African-American employees and gives philanthropically to organizations that help youth to pursue their dreams my ultimate intention is to uplift rather than degrade our community."[4]

Amy Dubois Barnett, editor in chief of *Ebony* magazine, spoke out about the incident in an editorial. In her view, it highlighted a larger problem with many rap lyrics:

> *Our boys are fed a hypnotic barrage of video images and lyrics that having a gun rather than an education is cool and that treating women like commodities is the way to be a man. . . . I'm officially tired of defending artists who seem to be willfully ignorant with regard to the damaging messages they spew for our kids to absorb.*[5]

Lil Wayne was hospitalized in March 2013 after having a seizure. Following his release, he issued a statement that he has epilepsy, and exhaustion brought on the most recent attack of seizures. Some journalists have speculated the seizures are linked to drug use, in particular to his habit of sipping codeine-laden purple drank, but the artist has not confirmed a link between his health issues and drugs.

GIVING BACK

Although controversy sometimes surrounds his music and his lifestyle, Lil Wayne has found ways to give back. In 2008, he started the One Family Foundation with the goal of helping urban youth achieve their dreams and become economically self sufficient. For the organization's launch, he asked students at Eleanor McMain Secondary School, which he attended until age 14, to design promotional materials. In return, he visited the school to speak to students. He encouraged them to go after their dreams, whatever they were, and be the best they could be at anything they did. When he was in prison, he bought an $11,000 wheelchair for the mother of a fan who had written to him. The fan had not even asked for help, but she had mentioned her mother's medical condition in her letters to Lil Wayne.

In 2012, Lil Wayne partnered with Mountain Dew to build a skate park in New Orleans' Ninth Ward, which was hit hard by Hurricane Katrina and had some difficulty recovering. Wayne had started skateboarding several years prior and decided to share the newfound passion with the kids of his former hometown. He and several professional skateboarders attended an opening

ON THE PRESIDENT'S MIND

President Barack Obama has mentioned Lil Wayne twice in public appearances. As a candidate in 2008, Obama encouraged kids at a campaign event in Georgia not to drop out of school. "You are probably not that good a rapper. Maybe you are the next Lil Wayne, but probably not, in which case you need to stay in school," he said.[6] Obama made a similar point in an address to a convention of the National Association for the Advancement of Colored People (NAACP) in 2009.

"They might think they've got a pretty jump shot or a pretty good flow, but our kids can't all aspire to be [basketball player] LeBron [James] or Lil Wayne. I want them aspiring to be scientists and engineers, doctors and teachers, not just ballers and rappers. I want them aspiring to be a Supreme Court justice. I want them aspiring to be president of the United States of America."[7] The president has also claimed to have Lil Wayne's music on his iPod.

Lil Wayne shows off on his skateboard in the New Orleans skate park he helped fund.

ceremony in September 2012. "I just want to help out my city, help out the people and the kids, give them something to do, something they haven't done before," he said. "It's always good to learn something new."[8]

|||||||||||||||||||||||||||||||||||||||||||||||||||||||||||

RETIREMENT?

As for his music career, Lil Wayne has said he would retire after *Tha Carter V*, although he hasn't said when he plans to release the next installment in that album series. "Carter V is my last album," he told an interviewer in November 2012. "Man, I've been rappin' since I was 8 years old. I'm 30 now, man. That's a long time, man."[9] Not everyone believes him though. One of his longtime producers said considering how much time Lil Wayne spends in the studio, it would be difficult to break the habit.

Whenever he decides to call it quits—if ever— his impact will remain. After getting his start as one of the youngest Hot Boys, he helped put southern hip-hop on the map and carved out his

> **"I don't like to stop. I believe you stop when you die."[10]**
>
> —*LIL WAYNE*

own unusual path to stardom through innovative marketing tactics and sometimes the sheer force of his personality. Lil Wayne will be remembered for his willingness to take risks and push the envelope as much as for his oversized personality and confidence.

||||||||||

Lil Wayne's fans will continue looking to the rapper for groundbreaking style and music.

TIMELINE

1982

Dwayne Michael Carter Jr. is born on September 27.

1991

Nine-year-old Dwayne meets Bryan and Ron Williams of Cash Money Records at a record signing.

1993

Dwayne officially signs with the record label Cash Money Records on May 13.

1998

Lil Wayne's first child, Reginae Carter, is born to his girlfriend, Antonia "Toya" Johnson on November 28.

1999

Lil Wayne's first solo album, *Tha Block Is Hot*, is released on November 2 and is soon certified platinum.

2000

Lights Out, Lil Wayne's second solo album, is released on December 19 and reaches gold status.

1993

Dwayne accidentally shoots himself near the heart while playing with a gun.

1997

On July 20, Lil Wayne's stepfather, Reginald "Rabbit" McDonald, is shot and killed.

1997

The Hot Boys' first album, *Get It How U Live!*, is released.

2002

With *500 Degreez*, Lil Wayne tries to prove he has the star power to keep the struggling Cash Money afloat.

2003

Lil Wayne starts his own label, Young Money Entertainment, under the umbrella of Cash Money.

2004

At 21 years old, Lil Wayne married Toya, the mother of his first child, on February 14.

TIMELINE

2004

Lil Wayne sees his popularity soar with *Tha Carter*, released on June 24, which features the hit single "Go DJ."

2005

Hurricane Katrina hits New Orleans on August 29, destroying much of Cash Money's assets.

2005

Tha Carter II, Lil Wayne's fifth album, is released on December 5.

2009

Lil Wayne welcomes two more children, Cameron Carter and Neal Carter, born two months apart on September 9 and November 30.

2010

On February 2, Lil Wayne's rock album *Rebirth* is released.

2010

On February 9, Lil Wayne begins serving a prison sentence after pleading guilty to attempted possession of a weapon.

2008

The much-anticipated *Tha Carter III* finally hits record stores on June 10, selling 1 million copies in its first week.

2008

Lil Wayne welcomes his second child, Dwayne Michael Carter III on October 22.

2009

Lil Wayne wins four Grammy Awards and performs a New Orleans tribute at the ceremony.

2010

From prison, Lil Wayne releases *I Am Not a Human Being* on September 27, his twenty-eighth birthday.

2011

Tha Carter IV is released on August 29 in the biggest debut of any hip-hop album since *Tha Carter III*.

2012

Lil Wayne tells a reporter in November he plans to retire after *Tha Carter V.*

GET THE SCOOP

FULL NAME

Dwayne Michael Carter Jr.

DATE OF BIRTH

September 27, 1982

PLACE OF BIRTH

New Orleans, Louisiana

MARRIAGE

Antonia "Toya" Johnson (2004–2006)

CHILDREN

Reginae Carter

Dwayne Michael Carter III

Cameron Carter

Neal Carter

SELECTED ALBUMS

Tha Block Is Hot (1999), *Tha Carter* (2004),
Tha Carter III (2008), *I Am Not a Human Being* (2010),
Tha Carter IV (2011)

SELECTED AWARDS

- Won the 2009 Grammy for Best Rap Album, Best Rap Solo Performance, Best Rap Performance by a Group, and Best Rap Song
- Won the 2011 BET Hip-Hop Award for Best Lyricist
- Won the 2012 *Billboard* Music Awards Top Male Artist

PHILANTHROPY

In 2008, Lil Wayne started the One Family Foundation to help urban youth achieve their dreams. He has also helped individual fans, buying a wheelchair for one fan's mother. Lil Wayne helped build a skate park in New Orleans' Ninth Ward to help the neighborhood recover after Hurricane Katrina.

"I just always expect the best because I'm a competitor and if I'm competing, then obviously I'm trying to be better in everything. I have no challengers—the challenger is everything—so I try to be the best."

—*LIL WAYNE*

GLOSSARY

Billboard—A music chart system used by the music recording industry to measure record popularity or sales.

bootleg—An illegally made and sold music CD or other recording.

chart—A weekly listing of songs or albums in order of popularity or record sales.

collaborate—To work together in order to create or produce a work, such as a song or album.

distribution—The marketing and merchandising of commodities.

explicit—Open in the depiction of nudity or sexuality.

freestyle—To perform verses on the spot rather than using prewritten lyrics.

Grammy Award—One of several awards the National Academy of Recording Arts and Sciences presents each year to honor musical achievement.

incarcerate—To put in prison.

incorrigible—Incapable of being corrected; unmanageable.

levee—An embankment for the prevention of flooding.

mixtape—In rap music, a compilation of unreleased tracks, freestyle rap music, and DJ mixes of songs.

platinum—A certification by the Recording Industry Association of America that an album has sold more than 1 million copies.

prolific—Very productive.

record label—A brand or trademark related to the marketing of music video and recordings.

reminiscent—Possessing a similar character to something else.

surrogate—Put in place of another.

ADDITIONAL RESOURCES

SELECTED BIBLIOGRAPHY

Binelli, Mark. "Life on Planet Wayne." *Rolling Stone* 16 Apr. 2009: 42–73. *Ebscohost*. Web. 1 May 2013.

Brown, Jake. *Lil Wayne (An Unauthorized Biography)*. Phoenix, AZ: Colossus, 2011. Print.

Serpick, Evan. "Lil Wayne Prepares His Post-Prison Comeback." *Rolling Stone* 11 Nov. 2010: 17–18. *Ebscohost*. Web. 1 May 2013.

Westhoff, Ben. *Dirty South: Outkast, Lil Wayne, Soulja Boy, and the Southern Rappers Who Reinvented Hip-Hop*. Chicago: Chicago Review Press, 2011. Print.

FURTHER READINGS

Cornish, Melanie. *The History of Hip Hop*. New York: Crabtree, 2009. Print.

Hill, Laban Carrick. *When the Beat Was Born: DJ Kool Herc and the Creation of Hip Hop*. New York: Roaring Brook, 2013. Print.

Lil Wayne. Costa Mesa, CA: Saddleback, 2013. Print.

WEB SITES

To learn more about Lil Wayne, visit ABDO Publishing Company online at **www.abdopublishing.com**. Web sites about Lil Wayne are featured on our Book Links page. These links are routinely monitored and updated to provide the most current information available.

PLACES TO VISIT

The Grammy Museum
800 W. Olympic Boulevard
Los Angeles, CA 90015-1300
213-765-6800
http://www.grammymuseum.org
The Grammy Museum features exhibits related to many genres of music.

New Orleans, Louisiana
1-800-672-6124
http://www.neworleanscvb.com
Visit the city of New Orleans, Louisiana, to see where southern bounce music was born and investigate a rich music tradition. Learn more about visiting the city and request brochures from the New Orleans Convention and Visitors Bureau.

SOURCE NOTES

CHAPTER 1. "BEST RAPPER ALIVE"

1. "Lil Wayne Can't Front on Fire." *MTV.com*. MTV Networks, 2007. Web. 19 May 2013.

2. Sasha Frere–Jones. "High and Mighty." *New Yorker* 13 Aug. 2007. *Ebscohost*. Web. 20 May 2013.

3. Ibid.

4. "Lil Wayne." *Encyclopædia Britannica*. Encyclopædia Britannica, 2013. Web. 1 May 2013.

5. Steve Jones. "Listen Up: Lil Wayne's 'Carter' Worth the Wait." *USA Today*. USA Today, 9 June 2008. Web. 13 May 2013.

6. "Lil Wayne Can't Front on Fire." *MTV.com*. MTV Networks, 2007. Web. 5 May 2013.

7. Sasha Frere–Jones. "High and Mighty." *New Yorker* 13 Aug. 2007. *Ebscohost*. Web. 1 May 2013.

8. Shaheem Reid. "Mixtapes: The Other Music Industry." *MTV.com*. MTV Networks, 2007. Web. 5 May 2013.

9. Ibid.

10. Ben Westhoff. *Dirty South: Outkast, Lil Wayne, Soulja Boy, and the Southern Rappers Who Reinvented Hip–Hop*. Chicago: Chicago Review, 2011. Print. 249.

11. Evan Serpick. "How Lil Wayne Became a Superstar." *Rolling Stone* 26 June 2008. 15–16. *Ebscohost*. Web. 1 May 2013.

12. Robert Levine. "Despite Leaks Online and File Sharing, Lil Wayne's New CD Is a Hit." *New York Times*. New York Times, 18 June 2008. Web. 1 May 2013.

13. Nekesa Mumbi Moody. "Lil Wayne's 'Tha Carter III' Sells 1 Million." *USA Today*. USA Today, 18 June 2008. Web. 13 May 2013.

14. Robert Levine. "Despite Leaks Online and File Sharing, Lil Wayne's New CD Is a Hit." *New York Times*. New York Times, 18 June 2008. Web. 1 May 2013.

15. Nekesa Mumbi Moody. "Lil Wayne's 'Tha Carter III' Sells 1 Million." *USA Today*. USA Today, 18 June 2008. Web. 13 May 2013.

16. Steve Jones. "Listen Up: Lil Wayne's 'Carter' Worth the Wait." *USA Today*. USA Today, 9 June 2008. Web. 13 May 2013.

17. Ben Westhoff. *Dirty South: Outkast, Lil Wayne, Soulja Boy, and the Southern Rappers Who Reinvented Hip–Hop*. Chicago: Chicago Review, 2011. Print. 252.

18. Robert Levine. "Despite Leaks Online and File Sharing, Lil Wayne's New CD Is a Hit." *New York Times*. New York Times, 18 June 2008. Web. 1 May 2013.

19. "Lil Wayne." *Encyclopædia Britannica*. Encyclopædia Britannica, 2013. Web. 1 May 2013.

CHAPTER 2. EARLY LIFE

1. Jake Brown. *Lil Wayne (An Unauthorized Biography)*. Phoenix, AZ: Colossus, 2011. Print. 28.

2. Ibid.

3. Mark Binelli. "Life on Planet Wayne." *Rolling Stone* 16 Apr. 2009. *Ebscohost*. Web. 1 May 2013.

4. Jake Brown. *Lil Wayne (An Unauthorized Biography)*. Phoenix, AZ: Colossus, 2011. Print. 29.

5. Ibid. 33–34.

6. Keith Spera. "Lil Wayne Goes Back to School." *Times-Picuyne*. NOLA Media Group, 23 Feb. 2008. Web. 1 May 2013.

CHAPTER 3. GROWING UP

1. Jake Brown. *Lil Wayne (An Unauthorized Biography)*. Phoenix, AZ: Colossus, 2011. Print. 34.

2. Ibid. 36.

3. Ibid. 36.

4. Mark Binelli. "Life on Planet Wayne." *Rolling Stone* 16 Apr. 2009. *Ebscohost*. Web. 1 May 2013.

5. Jake Brown. *Lil Wayne (An Unauthorized Biography)*. Phoenix, AZ: Colossus, 2011. Print. 80.

6. Mark Binelli. "Life on Planet Wayne." *Rolling Stone* 16 Apr. 2009. *Ebscohost*. Web. 1 May 2013.

7. Ibid.

8. Jake Brown. *Lil Wayne (An Unauthorized Biography)*. Phoenix, AZ: Colossus, 2011. Print. 37.

9. Ibid. 36.

10. Ibid. 43.

11. Mark Binelli. "Life on Planet Wayne." *Rolling Stone* 16 Apr. 2009. *Ebscohost*. Web. 1 May 2013.

CHAPTER 4. BREAKING OUT

1. "Lil Wayne Can't Front on Fire." *MTV.com*. MTV Networks, 2007. Web. 19 May 2013.

2. Jake Brown. *Lil Wayne (An Unauthorized Biography)*. Phoenix, AZ: Colossus, 2011. Print. 52.

3. Ibid. 55.

4. Jason Birchmeier. "Lights Out Review." *Allmusic*. Rovi Corp, 2013. Web. 13 May 2013.

5. Nathin Rabin. "Lights Out." *AV Club*. Onion Inc., 5 Dec. 2000. Web. 13 May 2013.

6. "500 Degreez." *LilWayneHQ.com*. Lil Wayne HQ, 2013. Web. 13 May 2013.

7. Steve Jones. "Maturity from Mario; 'Learning' from Lamya." *USA Today* 30 July 2002. *Ebscohost*. 13 May 2013.

CHAPTER 5. BREAKTHROUGH

1. Jake Brown. *Lil Wayne (An Unauthorized Biography)*. Phoenix, AZ: Colossus, 2011. Print. 61.

2. Joseph Patel. "Cash Money Dare You to Call It a Comeback." *MTV News*. Viacom. 10 Sept. 2003. Web. 15 May 2013.

3. Ben Westhoff. *Dirty South: Outkast, Lil Wayne, Soulja Boy, and the Southern Rappers Who Reinvented Hip–Hop*. Chicago: Chicago Review, 2011. Print. 250.

4. Jake Brown. *Lil Wayne (An Unauthorized Biography)*. Phoenix, AZ: Colossus, 2011. Print. 60.

5. Jon Pareles. "Rapper's Road to Pop." *New York Times*. New York Times, 10 June 2008. Web. 3 June 2013.

6. Jake Brown. *Lil Wayne (An Unauthorized Biography)*. Phoenix, AZ: Colossus, 2011. Print. 48.

CHAPTER 6. REBUILDING AND RESPECT

1. Jake Brown. *Lil Wayne (An Unauthorized Biography)*. Phoenix, AZ: Colossus, 2011. Print. 68.

2. Shaheem Reid. "Lil Wayne Working on Rebirth, Focusing on Young Money Label." *MTV News*. Viacom, 29 July 2009. Web. 19 May 2013.

3. "Lil Wayne Wants Respect for Southern Rap." *Today.com*. NBC News, 31 May 2006. Web. 17 May 2013.

4. Shaheem Reid. "Lil Big Man." *MTV.com*. MTV Networks, 2007. Web. 3 June 2013.

5. Tom Breihan. "Lil Wayne's 'Shooter': Best Song of the Year." *Village Voice*. Village Voice, 9 Dec. 2005. Web. 17 May 2013.

6. "Tha Carter II." *iTunes*. Apple Inc, 2013. Web. 15 May 2013.

7. Jake Brown. *Lil Wayne (An Unauthorized Biography)*. Phoenix, AZ: Colossus, 2011. Print. 77.

8. Ibid. 64.

9. Ibid. 73.

10. Ibid. 100.

11. Shaheem Reid. "Busy Lil Wayne Says 'I Am The Kobe Bryant Of Hip-Hop.'" *MTV News*. Viacom, 5 May 2006. Web. 15 July 2013.

12. Jake Brown. *Lil Wayne (An Unauthorized Biography)*. Phoenix, AZ: Colossus, 2011. Print. 112.

13. Jody Rosen. "Lil Wayne Tha Carter III." *Rolling Stone*. Rolling Stone, 26 June 2008. Web. 18 May 2013.

CHAPTER 7. NEW CHALLENGES

1. Jake Brown. *Lil Wayne (An Unauthorized Biography)*. Phoenix, AZ: Colossus, 2011. Print. 104.

2. Ibid. 155.

3. Ibid.

4. "Lil Wayne Awards and Nominations." *LilWayneHQ*. LilWayneHQ.com, 2013. Web. 15 May 2013.

5. Mariel Concepcion. "Producers Take Lil Wayne to the 'Prom.'" *Billboard*. Billboard, 27 Jan. 2009. Web. 20 May 2013.

6. Allison Stewart. "Album Review: Lil Wayne, 'Rebirth.'"*Washington Post*. Washington Post, 2 Feb. 2010. Web. 19 May 2013.

7. Jake Brown. *Lil Wayne (An Unauthorized Biography)*. Phoenix, AZ: Colossus, 2011. Print. 142.

8. Ibid. 122.

9. Chris Norris. "Lil Wayne Goes to Jail." *Rolling Stone* 18 Feb. 2010. *Ebscohost*. Web. 1 May 2013.

CHAPTER 8. ON THE INSIDE

1. Chris Norris. "Lil Wayne Goes to Jail." *Rolling Stone* 18 Feb. 2010. *Ebscohost*. Web. 1 May 2013.

2. Ibid.

3. Jake Brown. *Lil Wayne (An Unauthorized Biography)*. Phoenix, AZ: Colossus, 2011. Print. 148.

4. Jody Rosen. "Lil Wayne: I Am Not a Human Being." *Rolling Stone*. Rolling Stone, 29 Sept. 2010. Web. 20 May 2013.

5. Paris Hilton and Dmitri Ehrlich. "Lil Wayne." *Interview* Apr. 2011. 65–118. *Ebscohost*. Web. 1 May 2013.

6. Jake Brown. *Lil Wayne (An Unauthorized Biography)*. Phoenix, AZ: Colossus, 2011. Print. 161.

7. Keith Caulfield. "It's Official: Lil Wayne's Carter IV Debuts at Number 1 with 964,000 Sold." *Billboard*. Billboard, 6 Sept. 2011. Web. 22 May 2013.

8. Greg Kot. "Album Review: Lil Wayne, 'Tha Carter IV.'" *Chicago Tribune*. Chicago Tribune, 29 Aug. 2011. Web. 20 May 2013.

CHAPTER 9. NEW PURSUITS

1. Gil Kaufman. "T.I.'s And Lil Wayne's Daughters Start Group, OMG Girlz." *MTV News*. Viacom, 24 Nov. 2009. Web. 15 July 2013.

2. Hattie Collins. "Wayne's World." *Guardian*. Guardian News, 7 June 2008. Web. 19 May 2013.

3. "PepsiCo Drops Lil Wayne over Emmett Till Controversy." *Huff Post Pop Culture*. Huff Post Multicultural, 3 May 2013. Web. 20 May 2013.

4. "Lil Wayne Emmett Till Lyric: Rapper Issues Apology to Till Family." *Huff Post Pop Culture*. Huff Post Multicultural, 1 May 2013. Web. 20 May 2013.

5. Amy Dubois Barnett. "Lil Wayne, What Were You Thinking?" *Ebony* Apr. 2013. 16. *Ebscohost*. Web. 1 May 2013.

6. "Barack Obama References Lil Wayne." *Prefix*. Prefix, 9 July 2008. Web. 19 May 2013.

7. Sheryl Gay Stolberg. "Obama Gives Fiery Address at NAACP." *New York Times*. New York Times, 16 July 2009. Web. 19 May 2013.

8. "Lil Wayne Opens Skatepark in New Orleans." *AP Financial News* 27 Sept. 2012. *Ebscohost*. Web. 1 May 2013.

9. Rob Markman. "Will Lil Wayne Really Retire After Carter V?" *MTV News*. Viacom, 29 Mar. 2013. Web. 24 May 2013.

10. Chris Norris. "Lil Wayne Goes to Jail." *Rolling Stone* 18 Feb. 2010. Ebscohost. Web. 1 May 2013.

INDEX

ABOUT THE AUTHOR

Erika Wittekind is a freelance writer and editor living in Madison, Wisconsin. She has written more than half a dozen books for children and young adults. In 2002, she graduated from Bradley University with a bachelor's degree in journalism and political science.